LISTEN. THINK. SPEAK.

by Wassila Hachchi

Table of Contents

"In the 21st century we need to create conscious conversations that make a difference in the world. Wassila has created the answers for that. Powerful dialogue changes communities, families, and relationships. This book should be in every business and every family home."

Lisa Nichols

CEO Motivating The Masses

What do you feel and see when you're on the internet? Millions and millions of words exploding everywhere. People are constantly talking. But to what purpose? Are we learning anything from one another? Are we openly sharing our beliefs, or are we just talking? And aren't we missing a real opportunity to grow and step into our power to make a difference?

Now is the time to listen, think and then speak. And that is finally possible. Dialogue Digital is my dream and vision that has come to fruition. Dialogue Digital is an online platform where people can come together for intelligent conversations. But let me first share my story.

A LIFE IN SERVICE

I am Wassila Hachchi. I feel like I've lived many lives while one common thread runs throughout my 36 years: I always lived my life in service. But why? I now know that I lived my life of service to be accepted.

As a young child, I served in order to make my parents proud. When I grew older, I started serving my community by becoming a role model as a successful second-generation child of Moroccan immigrants in my country, the Netherlands. Why? Because in every country in the world there is a minority group of immigrants that somehow continues to be labeled and stigmatized. In the Netherlands, that's the Moroccan immigrant community. Whether this is right or not, it was my reality. From this perspective I experienced life, and it made my hunger for acceptance grow. So I continued serving, first in the military by joining the Royal Dutch Navy after graduating with a Master's degree in Business Administration at the Erasmus University in Rotterdam.

The Royal Dutch Navy was the first place I experienced the feeling of acceptance as a Dutch. Of course, this happened after first proving myself both mentally and physically. You see, you have to earn the uniform and title of military officer. But looking back at that time, I realize how unique that experience was. Everybody comes in and turns in all their personal stuff, gets the same haircut and has to show what value they uniquely add to the team. You're being accepted based on that value. It meant so much to me because it was the first time I really felt like I belong in the Netherlands. The Netherlands is my country, and I realized how long it took me to genuinely experience that feeling. This feeling motivated me to serve my country more. After 4 years in the military it was time for change.

Next I became a government official, and even though I held an important position, my need to be accepted returned. I've always tried to remember that real sense of acceptance I felt at the Navy, but apparently it wasn't sustainable. I felt I had to prove myself all over again outside the military world. I continued my work in public service. I worked for the Ministry of Economic Affairs and the Ministry of Defense, and I even received an award for outstanding performances. I remember that evening when I received the award. It was after I had given a speech from my core, right from the heart. It was a speech about how important it is to be yourself and therefore naturally inspire others. Almost 10 years ago I still remember my words in that speech, and I still feel the emotions I felt at that moment sharing them because it was a call for acceptance. My whole life I was unconsciously serving to feel accepted. There was this gap inside of me and it was keeping me restless. By winning this award, I became a role model for people in public service and even an ambassador to attract others to become a civil servant.

But even with that award in my hand and hundreds of congratulations it was not enough - I wanted more. My hunger for acceptance wasn't gone. Despite one promotion after another, the hunger was still there. I now see what was really going on, it was my underlying sense that I was not enough, even though I was being my authentic self. In the meantime, I continued doing what I did best: serving. I wanted to serve more. I wanted to play bigger, so I needed to take being in service to the next level.

Finally, I thought that I found the perfect forum to take my dedication to serve to the next level - by entering politics where I could make a real difference. This time I was totally exposed and vulnerable and I knew that I could either be an advocate or target. For me it was my bigger level of serving. But just when I expected to feel like I was doing enough, I experienced not feeling accepted more than ever before in my life. So how did I deal with this?

My survival strategy was to excel in everything I did and to be fully dedicated to my task as a representative. I did this because that's what I wanted in my core, to be a representative for my country and my people. Despite the boxes others tried to put me in, the Moroccan or Dutch box, I did politics like I did anything else: very dutifully. I obeyed the rules. Both the written and unwritten ones. I obeyed the "this is how we do it" rules even when those rules didn't serve me. Without judgment or blaming others - I was responsible. I followed what others were telling me to do and I held myself in judgment.

The longer I was in politics, the more I felt like I was losing myself. I felt like I was losing my vulnerability and the fearlessness that has always defined who I was. Most importantly, I felt like I was losing my faith in politics, and in me. While on the outside, I looked like the flawless, totally dedicated politician. And again, there is no judgment or blaming. I'm responsible. No one took Wassila away from me. I gave her away. No one required that I lose my vulnerability, I gave it away. No one asked me to stop being fearless; I just started being more fearful of not being accepted. No one asked me to lose my faith. I don't even know when I lost it. I just woke up one morning and I lost it as if I had lost my shoes. I couldn't find my faith. I had lost faith in the political system I was once honored to be part of and that I had joined to serve. It was right then, in this intense time of deep inner sadness that I learned to listen - not to those around me but to my inner voice and understanding who I truly was and what was driving me in life. I found my calling, or maybe it found me.

ACCEPTANCE AND APPROVAL

After 3 years in the political arena I started seeing life from a different perspective. As I look around, I saw a whole bunch of people in politics that were "speaking" their message without a real dialogue with one another. At that time politicians were struggling with several social issues, such as radicalization among Muslim youngsters. Their only solution was to take away their passports or say "let them die in Syria". They were in total denial that they were our youngsters - second and third generation sons and daughters of immigrants, and some even native Dutch. Here is where the idea for an online platform to have intelligent conversations with people instead of just talking about people was born: I named it Dialogue Digital.

Dialogue Digital is an opportunity to really take all of the conversations and debates that are happening, especially on the Internet, to the next level. I wanted to create a platform to help people have meaningful conversations with one another. Social change is needed. While I was active in politics, I realized that social change starts from outside the political system, not from within. I didn't know how to realize this, but I decided to continue listening deep within me, think about what deep within me wants to emerge and act on it. I started sharing with people this idea of Dialogue Digital that I had, and slowly but surely I found partners to make this idea concrete.

After struggling through four more years serving as a "dedicated" Member of Parliament, I knew, thanks to the passion I had for Dialogue Digital, it was time to move outside of what I was doing. I knew that the changes that I needed to find out were changes that needed to happen inside of me. As I made this commitment, I began to find a new energy. I began to find myself again and see my faith re-emerge. You see, politics is very energy consuming. It's easy to lose yourself in it, to lose your voice and to lose your ability to listen to what people want. Dialogue Digital became my lifeline and source of renewed energy.

Even though I had decided in January 2015 that I was going to leave politics, I didn't leave immediately for 101 reasons, or may just 3. In the end, it all came down to one thing: my hunger for acceptance was still alive and kicking. While I had my energy back, I knew that I needed to leave, but I didn't feel like I had the approval to leave. I've always been dedicated, first as a little girl, then as a woman, as a military official, in public service and now in politics, but I knew I had to step out and focus on what was driving me. I needed to take Dialogue Digital further. It was a huge step to leave the Parliament, and again I was looking for that approval from someone before I was finally able to make the change I knew I needed to make. Sound familiar? Do you ever hear inside of you that voice that tells you the next step you should make, but instead of following that voice of change inside of yourself you wait for the approval of someone else?

During this time as I was waiting for approval, I actually received two job opportunities. But I still didn't leave. In the meantime, my drive to actualize Dialogue Digital was growing. Every single day it became clearer to me that it was my calling in life.

AFTER LISTENING AND THINKING I STARTED SPEAKING

All my efforts took place in my few spare hours I had each day, in addition to my full time position as a Member of Parliament. The reality was that I needed the energy that Dialogue Digital provided to continue working in the political arena. As word spread about Dialogue Digital, I was asked to give a talk at TEDX Amsterdam Women. I also created funds to create Dialogue Digital, through a crowd funding campaign I initiated. Although I was a bit disappointed in the lack of support from my Dutch political and media networks, with a few exceptions, my fire for Dialogue Digital kept on growing. And could you believe I garnered support from the other side of the ocean, the United States? By the end of 2015 and as a result of Dialogue Digital's successful crowd funding campaign, I received an invitation to get involved with the Hillary Clinton campaign. While it wasn't a concrete job offer, it was concrete enough for me to hear my inner voice loud and clear: if people in the United States - the land of the brave - embraces Dialogue Digital, the rest will surely follow. How do I know this? The Netherlands has always been a follower of the Americans in every issue and matter. I have experienced it up close as a Member of Parliament. We rely on the United States. So this opportunity in the States was concrete enough for me to leap. I was ready to leap, but I was also scared and still waiting for approval.

WILLING TO FIGHT

In January 7th 2016, just after my birthday, something happened while I was out jogging in the early morning. I often jog in my hometown forest. I do it to help me meditate and to focus. When I commune with nature, I feel God's presence. I feel the permission to open my heart, and to allow my strength to get back in. But this particular morning I had questions. Have you ever had questions like "what should I do?" "I want to take the opportunity, but am I strong enough?" "What would people say?" See I had all these questions while being a public figure. "What story would they tell?" "Will it all work out in the States? This opportunity to join and experience the Hillary Clinton campaign is a once in a lifetime chance!" The United States of America, the land of those who dream big and play big. I wanted to own it, harness hit, hold on to it, embody it, and live it so I can come back home with an ever stronger fearlessness and faith, and pass it on in the Netherlands. But there were so many questions, and I kept on firing them at God. I asked for guidance, help, and protection. "Please God, give me courage and strength so I can go through anything." I did all of this while I was jogging non-stop for almost 45 minutes.

As I was jogging and talking to God asking Him what I should do, I saw an energy. I looked into the distance and noticed a dark animal running toward me at a lightning speed, and getting closer to me as each and every second passed. The image got sharper. I noticed it was a dog. Suddenly I hear panic stricken voices yelling "Come back! Come back! Get over here!", I don't remember the name of the dog, but I'll call it Killer. "Get over here, Killer!" I noticed Killer is not turning around. He was coming for me. Now that I was locked on Killer, I realized Killer was locked on me. In an instant, all of my fears shifted from leaving the Parliament, from leaving my country, from leaving my family, from being accepted in the States, from everything. All my fears shifted from what to do, what will they say about me, and what will they write about me. All of my fears shifted to one of survival – to how to fight Killer. Killer's instinct was to rip through my body. That was his intention, and he came at me full sprint. But something rose in me that I know we have in all of us. Something was required to come out of me that I didn't know I had. The minutes between the owners of that dog being able to run and catch their dog and stop him were the longest minutes of my life. But in those minutes, I learned how to fight for me. I learned how to fight for my calling. It was worth fighting a vicious and aggressive Belgian Shepherd. For minutes I was fighting him off, all of my drive to live came to the surface. The blessing was that long after they got Killer away from me, I knew that I was willing to fight for my calling and to be all of who I truly am. At that very moment, even after receiving a bite on my arm and a few scratches on my body as I was fighting Killer off, I actually found the answer to all of my questions.

KEEPING SILENT

Finally, I gave notice that I was relinquishing my seat in Parliament early – I had one year to go. And for the first time in my life I did what I knew I had to do, without anyone's approval and I felt great because of that. My colleagues in Parliament were shocked because like I said, from the outside I had been the dedicated politician. Nobody had any idea of the daily inner struggles I endured day after day for almost 6 years. Because of how well I had done, the media was thrilled to have my resignations as the next exciting and juicy issue to exploit. They covered my leaving amazingly well. As the news of my decision to leave first brake, people were excited to hear about my opportunity to work within the Hillary Clinton campaign and all that was going on in my life. I was also surprised just how encouraging people actually were. I was getting texts, calls and notes from a wide spectrum of people congratulating me. Throughout this transition I felt surprisingly calm inside. It felt like I was looking at my own life from a distance and seeing what was happening without it really affecting me. I was strong and completely at peace within myself. I never felt like that before. I knew that creating Dialogue Digital and having this opportunity in the United States was going to take me into my destiny. What other people thought about me no longer mattered. It was from this point of clarity that I was able to ignore the media's relentless pursuit for "the inside scoop". My hunger for acceptance was finally gone. I felt deep within me the acceptance I was longing for since I was a little girl, a woman, in the military, a civil servant and a politician - my own acceptance. That's all I needed. I was convicted of what I needed to do and no one could stop me anymore.

A couple of days after the announcement broke, the media wanted to know more. They asked questions like, "Why was she leaving? What was the problem in the party? Who did she have troubles with?" They were all digging in because that's their job. They wanted me to react so they could get some juicy answers, as speculation began spurring around me – one falsehood feeding the next - but I kept silent. You see, in life we have to learn how to listen, think and then speak, as opposed to reacting right away without thinking. I knew within me that this wasn't the time for me to make comments. I just needed to keep silent. In my family, I was raised with values, and one of them is to not talk bad about others. I was taught to always take responsibility in any situation. In this case, I also didn't really feel like there was anybody I needed to blame. It was my own choice. I took full responsibility because I felt the power within me to be doing what I was getting ready to do, take the step into what I was called to do. It helped me realize that I had the power, not just to speak out, but also to not respond to certain statements that people make.

A MOVEMENT FOR CHANGE

The next day I arrived in New York and went directly to the Hillary Clinton campaign headquarters in Brooklyn. Immediately, everyone was like, "It's her! It's her!" People already knew who I was and had expectations of my involvement in the campaign. I have to admit that I was really disappointed and even angry with the media in the Netherlands for casting a negative shadow as to my involvement in the campaign, which created a short term stigma that didn't serve anybody. But looking back, it was a blessing in disguise. Because I traveled with the campaign throughout many States and I had the pleasure of talking to both Hillary supporters as well as Bernie and Trump people. I got to understand what was happening in the country during this most divisive presidential race. I saw this on the ground, and not from the mainstream media or from a fancy office in the headquarters in Brooklyn, but first hand from the American people.

As a result, I learned a lot of things about how campaigns are organized and run in the United States. I gained a first-hand insight into the inner working of both the Democratic and the Republican parties. What struck me is that the same thing was happening in and around both parties. Both parties experienced the same social unrest during their campaign. There was a movement happening — a movement for change.

After spending time in different states, one thing became clear regardless, people wanted change. They were tired of the establishment and were looking for radical change. It felt stronger than the hope for change the country felt when they elected President Obama. The only difference between the Democrats and Republicans really ended up being that though the Democrats ignored this voice calling for change and nominated Hillary, while the Republicans had nominated Trump and they had - despite the troubles - embraced that anti-establishment sentiment that was so resounding in the people that I was meeting.

MORE THAN READY

I remember sitting there on Election Day in Nevada in Hillary's headquarters with a big group of amazing staffers I had gotten to know better during my time in several States. There was a sense of surprise as the election went on. The media perception had been telling us all along that the outcome was obvious – Hillary would win hands down. At the end of the day, although I didn't really want to see Donald Trump win, I understood why he did.

Over the course of this last part of the year I finally had time to focus all of my attention on realizing my vision to create an online platform for intelligent dialogue. I dove into creating Dialogue Digital working with my coach, Lisa Nichols. Lisa is one of the world's most-requested motivational speakers, media personality and corporate CEO whose global platform reaches 30 million people. She is helping me create this movement strategically - one step at the time. Why? Because we both really want all of us work together in order to gain influence on social issues that matter to us. I want us to create together a platform where intelligent conversations happen and build an online community that will drive social change. For example, just imagine the topic global warming – now envision a scientist in China, an economist in the United States, a former ambassador and a school teacher could actually collaborate and come up with a solution for a new product, process or proposal for legislature and even generate relevant support to get this legislature passed.

WHAT IT WILL TAKE

We can effect change at a grass root level where – thanks to the internet – distance and official qualifications aren't need to participate creating a true sense of democracy through collaboration, compassion and meaningful conversations. We need to stop just voting for politicians and sitting back waiting for them to solve our problems. Instead we need to work together. We need to create dialogue to effect meaningful change. It's time for us to wake up: we are the leaders. We need to stop relying on politicians to create change. While they are supposed to serve us, we need to hold them accountable in order to ensure that they take action to find solutions.

My insights taught me the real value of listening, taking time to really think and being impeccable with my word. I have learned that there are times when the best thing to do is just to shut up and listen, rather than filling the Internet up with more "speaking without thought." The people in control of the media tell us what to believe and they manipulate our minds like puppets, which means in whatever way they want. If they want us to hate someone, they spread a gossip all around, and the lies work their magic. We need to stop being puppets. We need to first listen, think and then speak. More and more people are becoming aware and awake. Are you?

Let's work together and let us - the people - lead so politicians become true servants. After the election, what I really realized is that people are more than ready for this. They are ready for Dialogue Digital.

HOW DIALOGUE DIGITAL WORKS

So, how does this work? Here are the five pillars on which Dialogue Digital is built and is based on the need to:

Understand and embrace dialogue

Create and protect a safe space for dialogue

Master listening

Bring the fullness of yourself to the dialogue and encourage others to bring theirs

Be resilient

To elaborate, **first** of all we need to be aware that dialogue is not a conversation or debate. Dialogue starts with an intention. The intention is to be genuinely open to another person. You're aware of different perspectives and no matter what your perception is, it's still a perception, not the ultimate truth.

Secondly, true dialogue cannot occur without a safe space. What is a safe space? It's a space where people can be themselves and express their ideas without fear of being judged. In a safe space there can never be repercussions. You have to know that what you share is not going to be held against you in any way in the future. Unconditional love is another element of a safe space - being aware that we are all human beings and that we are connected is the source of love. It creates energy in which people dare to be their true selves and open up. Nobody is perfect and we all have our ugly sides.

Thirdly, dialogue begins by listening. It begins with hearing what the other person is saying, and then truly taking the time to genuinely think about what they are saying rather than just needing to make your own point be known. We need to actually listen, take it in and then think about it. We have to be willing to do something with this new information that we've heard. After you've thought it through carefully, then it is time to open your mouth and speak.

The **fourth** element to truly create a Dialogue Digital that grows beyond each person listening to the others' voice, thinking about what they're saying and also speaking their truth is: bringing in the fullness of yourself and encourage others to bring in theirs. I spent my life trying hard to do whatever I could to be accepted. But now, what I've realized is that I don't need acceptance from others. What I need to be is who I truly am. That's how you find your calling, or better yet, it will find you. Accept your calling. It's not somebody else's or somebody outside of you that you're looking for. The only person that you need acceptance from is yourself. When you truly and completely embrace who you are, you can get to a place where you value what you have to contribute. Bringing the fullness of ourselves to the dialogue, is what makes Dialogue Digital effective. The goal is to create conversations on Dialogue Digital that lead to action, because accepting your calling means that you are willing to take action.

The **fifth** and final element of making this work is resilience. You have to be willing to stand for what you believe in. Just like with the dog, Killer, I had to stand my ground and be willing to fight him. You have to be resilient enough to stand your ground, speak your truth and fight for the change that you know you want in life despite any hurdle you encounter on your way.

IT STARTS WITH YOU

You won't lose yourself by being vulnerable, it means simply being transparent. Fearless means embracing courage as your opportunity in life. You only lose your faith when you stop standing for what you believe in. Now is the time that we surprise each other with what we have to share by being fearless, open and honest with each other. I invite you to have faith, because no matter how it looks, what you know in your belly and your soul is all that matters. Your calling is all that matters, and that's where your faith lives. That's who you are. Have faith in what you believe in. Listen to that deep inner voice inside of you. Then do something with it. Now is your time. You have the opportunity for your voice to be heard. It all starts from your willingness to listen, think and speak because your voice has value. Its value comes when you connect with others and come together to drive social change.

As a social entrepreneur, what I want more than anything else is to be the catalyst that helps drive the changes that we so desperately need. It starts with people just like you, people who are willing to connect with each other to influence the course of society and get a greater and deeper perspective on social issues. As we all come together in Dialogue Digital, we will grow together. As we listen, think and speak, we will enhance one another, share our truths and make our world a better place. I invite you all to join Dialogue Digital today, because together we can really affect change.

" The most intense fight a human will ever have is between the person they are and the person they are capable of becoming."

- Jerald "Coach Jae" Lewis

PEOPLE WHO INSPIRED THE CREATION OF THIS BOOK

People you meet on your journey present a lesson for you. I have heard that line many times in my life. This year, 2016, I have learned to live by it every day – moment by moment. By embracing my calling and acting on it, I have met people who inspire me. In this chapter, I introduce to you three of these people and their service in this world.

TONY'S CHOCOLONELY
– HENK JAN BELTMAN

The founder of <u>Tony's Chocolonely</u> - a chocolate company – woke up one day to discover that the thriving chocolate industry was fueled by slaves often as young as 6 years. From its start Tony's Chocolonely has one vision: no more slavery in the chocolate industry worldwide. Henk Jan Beltman is - as he likes to be called - the Chief Chocolate Officer. He and his team lead by example and activate industry, politics and consumers to bring about change. Henk Jan is an award winning entrepreneur, not only for his efforts for 100%

slave free chocolate, but for proving that success and ideals go well together. For me Henk Jan is an angel in disguise. He supported me to bring Dialogue Digital's crowd funding to success. He always shows up at the right time and place, and he believed in me and Dialogue Digital unconditionally. You can read more about Tony's Chocolonely on their website: www.tonyschocolonely.com

MOTIVATING THE MASSES – LISA NICHOLS

Motivating the Masses is a transformational company and is led by two extraordinary women, Lisa Nichols and Susie Carder. They inspire me to grow, while at the same time holding on to my authenticity in order to excel as a social entrepreneur. They demonstrate leadership in its purest and rarest nature, especially in the sober Netherlands. I would have never heard of Motivating the Masses if it wasn't for Lisa. During my stay in California we've met and it was a story Lisa shared with me that convinced me that she is the coach I was looking for - the person who is 10 or more steps ahead of you and is your example in every kind of way. Lisa shared a story about her past in which she felt a core shaking feeling deep in her stomach. It made her run out of the room she was in with other people and she cried ugly alone in the bathroom. I've experienced the exact same feeling in October 2015, while I was in the Parliament attending a political group meeting. Her description of the feeling was spot on. Right then and there I choose her as my coach. Months afterwards, I feel blessed to share my experiences, my lessons and my love for Lisa and her team. To learn more about Lisa you can read her many books and visit www.motivatingthemasses.com

MINDVALLEY
– VISHEN LAKHIANI

Embracing my social entrepreneurship fully all started with one book, The Code of The Extraordinary Mind by Vishen Lakhiani. When I finished reading it in one day I sent Vishen an email with compliments. He replied instantly with thoughtful words and he invited me to join A-Fest, an invite-only community of more than 1000 extraordinary people from more than 40 different countries who come together to connect, grow, support each other, and learn from the world's best teachers. Vishen's Mindvalley incubates and grows businesses that innovate on transformational education dedicated to unleashing humanity's greatest potential. Check their website at **www.mindvalley.com**

LISTEN. THINK. SPEAK.

I share with you these people and their incredible work on this planet so they can be an inspiration for you too. And you can find your own inspirators. Nobody achieves success on their own. It starts with looking for, finding and surrounding yourself with people who get it. You are not alone. Get together, work together and make the changes you want to see in your life, your society and your world. As a starting social entrepreneur I felt alone for too long while I was actually never alone. I look forward to meeting you online.